Classic Boats of the West Country

Drawing on our maritime tradition

Ian Heard

Bossiney Books·Launceston

Dedicated to the memory of my father, Terry Heard, for his vision and the legacy he has left us all

Grateful thanks go to all the enthusiastic contributors who have helped me with their stories, references and hospitality in the making of this book, notably the owners of many of the boats featured – *Kathleen and May, Andorra, Edith, Guide Me* and *Tomboy, Bessie Ellen, Max, Little Mint* and the Brixham Trawlers – and Morwellham and Tamar Valley Trust, and Peter Allington of the National Maritime Museum, Cotehele. Special thanks go to Mike Atfield, Robert Dern of the Sea Chest Bookshop, Alan Abbott of the Beer Luggers Club, Marcus Lewis of the Fowey Troy Class, the owners of Mylor Yacht Harbour for letting me see the new Sunbeam, and John Bawden of Newquay Rowing Club for revealing their hidden treasures.

Finally, my thanks to Eve, for always being there.

The front cover shows the *Bessie Ellen* (see page 32) now relaunched

This paperback edition published 2008 by Bossiney Books Ltd, Langore, Launceston, Cornwall PL15 8LD
First published 2002 by Bossiney Books

ISBN 978-1-906474-12-6

Printed in China

It's only in recent times that 'classic boat' has become a familiar term. Boats were just 'old boats' and the concept of 'classic' applied to grand stuff like music and art.

However, those old boats and the boatmen of the south west have left an indelible legacy. Although many wooden ships have succumbed to the mudbanks, a modest number are enjoying a magnificent revival of our traditional craft. There's also a growing fascination with the trades which supported the maritime industries – from boat building to sail making – and even a renewed interest in sea-shanty singing. Modern designers and boat builders are also looking to the past for inspiration, building not just replicas, but new craft in new materials. The lug rig, once consigned to history, is a perfect example of how windward ability and four-sided sails need not be strangers.

There are now weekend rallies during the summer months, where enthusiastic owners can show off their lovingly restored vessels and crews can compete in friendly racing. One can see at close hand original examples of some of our great working boats, survivors from the age of sail that faded from view not that long ago. The diarist Francis Kilvert once remarked that he couldn't see the horizon for the masts of ships anchored in Falmouth's Carrick Roads and there are old photographs of harbours crowded with ketches, hookers, quay punts, toshers and picaroons. Other boats with even older names like polaccas and muffies are lumped together with their big sisters into the phrase 'tall ships', another modern expression that would be lost on our forefathers.

This book is an introduction to those classic boats. It's a sketchbook and only scratches the surface of a subject that could easily become a lifetime's study. I have tried to concentrate on authentic originals, but I've included some extensive rebuilds that were too good to leave out. I also include some beautiful 'class' racing designs that have developed organically, and some elegant gentlemen's yachts from an age when straw hats and blue blazers were *de rigueur*.

Lastly, this book is intended to be an interesting diversion – to encourage the reader to look again, and invite them to make contact with the humble working boats of Britain that helped found our maritime nation.

Bristol Channel Pilot Cutters

There are fewer than twenty of these famous craft sailing today. At the turn of the twentieth century there were over one hundred 'skiffs' carving the waters of the Bristol Channel and the western approaches. Their role was primarily to search out the returning cargo ships and provide them with a local pilot whose job was to guide the ships safely back to port. They would live out in the Atlantic to the south west of Ireland and patrol the seas from Liverpool around Land's End to Start Point. Some south coast ports had pilots too (often there were pilots in families for generations), including Plymouth and Falmouth which boasted numerous elegant cutters now long since gone. The Isles of Scilly had up to a dozen cutters, as the islands were the first landfall for ships running home.

The cutter's seaworthiness is legendary and there are several modern replicas to be found sailing around the south west. Many cruise as yachts and go much further afield.

The Barry pilot cutter *Cornubia* was built in Polruan in Cornwall by J Slade and Son and was launched in 1911. She seems to have worked successfully until 1920 when she was sold as a yacht and later renamed *Hirta* by one Scottish owner. She spent the war years at a sailing school on the Isle of Bute and in more recent years has crossed the Atlantic several times as well as featuring in a BBC series and in books and articles written by her last owner.

Hirta is currently undergoing a major refit in Gloucester, but will no doubt soon be seen kicking up her heels as she closes her first century.

Kathleen and May

The three tall masts of the schooner *Kathleen and May* tower over the mudbanks of the river Torridge opposite Bideford. She was the last working merchant schooner to be registered at a port in the United Kingdom, and the last to earn her living at sea. She was built at Connah's Quay on the Dee in North Wales in 1900 and was originally named *Lizzie May*. At almost 100 ft long she could carry about 250 tons of cargo. The ship worked hard in the coastal trade, carrying bulk items such as coal, china clay, cement and bricks, fertilisers and grain between ports around the British Isles.

In 1908 she was sold to Martin J Fleming of Youghal in the Irish Republic and was registered at Cork. Her name was changed to *Kathleen and May* and she sailed from Youghal for twenty-three years. In 1931 she was sold to Captain William Jewell of Appledore in north Devon and carried coal from Mersey to the south coast right through the war. A new engine was fitted and her hatches were enlarged. Her rig was also modified to give her a reduced sail wardrobe as a motor vessel with sails. She continued to work up to 1960 when the then skipper Tom Jewell retired her from service.

She slowly declined as old boats do, but was spotted on the Torridge by the newly formed Maritime Trust in 1970. They rightly felt her to be an important example and set about saving her. Work was carried out in Appledore and Cremyll and she was moored in Sutton harbour, Plymouth, until 1978, when she was taken to St Katherine's Dock, London, as part of the historic ships collection. She was allowed to deteriorate to a state where she was closed to the public and towed to Gloucester where she was discovered by Bideford businessman Steve Clarke, who subsequently bought her and towed the hull back to his home town and her old home port in north Devon. She was to be restored as the focal point in the regeneration of the town but it was clear as repair work progressed that major surgery was required. Over the next four years, with hard work and not inconsiderable investment, Mr Clarke and his team slowly brought *Kathleen and May* back from the brink, and the historic vessel was finally relaunched in May 2001.

That summer, plans unfolded to take her to sea once more. One August morning, *Kathleen and May* slipped her mooring alongside the wharf at East-the-Water, and later slid out on the evening tide bound for Appledore and then Ireland. Once safely at sea and following trials around Lundy Island, they triumphantly crossed the Irish Sea to Youghal in twenty hours. One can only guess at how many times she had made that journey in the past.

Newquay Pilot Gigs

Deep within the cave-like cellars beneath the streets of Newquay lies a treasure spanning almost two hundred years and one that palpably illustrates our on-going relationship with the sea. To run your hands along the gunnels of the gig *Newquay* is to make real contact with an England before the battle of Waterloo. Built by William Peters of St Mawes, she dates from 1812.

The *Dove* dates from 1820, and the sleek, pale blue *Treffry* was built in 1838. Remarkably, these slender rowing boats are still actively raced throughout the summer and provide a spectacle for all to enjoy. In a museum, they would be behind glass. *Treffry* is regarded as particularly special, and was reckoned by the Peters family to be the best they ever built. Legend says she was not painted, but polished with linseed oil before being rowed upriver to Truro, and then carried by hand to Newquay some 12 miles away.

Like the pilot cutters, the gigs conveyed a pilot and would be rowed out into the western approaches to await the home-bound sailing ships. Their speed and agility made them a notorious favourite of smugglers. In fact, they became so effective that eventually the number of oars was restricted and gigs over 28 ft were banned by Act of Parliament. Only the Isles of Scilly were allowed bigger boats with six oars – they had their day jobs to think of, after all!

gig under sail

The gigs were also equipped with mains'l and mizzen and are still built with tack hooks in their forward quarters. Sails were needed for their work downwind, often up to 120 miles out at sea. One Peters gig, *Bonnet* (1830), is reputed to have made the passage from Scilly to France twenty-five times. She still races today, and the regattas among the rocks and islands are something to behold.

Quiet Mooring

Penzance lugger *Andorra* quietly stems the tide on the Fowey river. This boat is typical of Mount's Bay fishing boats and crabbers which used to exist in large numbers. The dipping lug rig was once standard among the inshore craft and would have looked much the same on the half-decked pilchard drivers. So it is on the even bigger luggers like *Guide Me* and *Our Daddy*, now also enjoying a revival. The smaller luggers were almost always open boats and could be found all along the coast, pot hauling and lining for mackerel and bass.

Andorra's history is unknown before 1971 when she was found as a motor boat, and registered as PZ288 based in Newlyn. By 1986, however, while suffering hard times, one of her legs had buckled beneath her and she was filling with green water with every tide. She was duly rescued and taken to Hampshire for a refit that included re-installing a mast and sails. In 1989 *Andorra* was purchased by her present owner who undertook further restoration with larch decks and low bulwarks before coming back to the west country. He also returned her rig to the more authentic dipping lug.

She was first moored at Weir Quay on the river Tamar before moving downstream to her present moorings at Cargreen. This is an historic part of the old river. Once a thriving industrial area, it's now a quiet place, the haunt of white egrets and cruising yachts. *Andorra* too is well travelled for a small boat and her skipper cruises her as far as the Isles of Scilly. She is also a familiar sight at summer rallies and festivals.

Falmouth Working Boats

No one can fail to be bowled over by the sight of the Falmouth working boats as they surge through the moorings off Flushing or St Mawes, or in one of the other weekly regattas that take place during the summer. With their colourful tops'ls and liveried crews, they have created one of the most memorable sights on the water.

More important, though, is the fact that many of these craft are still dredging boats, and are the last fleet to work purely under sail almost anywhere (engines were banned from use under a bylaw in 1868). During the winter months, working boats can be found braving harsh weather to dredge the oysters on the river Fal. Their complicated looking gaff rig comes into its own as mains'ls are scandalised (their peaks are lowered away), and their tiny scraps of working headsails billow away to leeward. The racing summer crew is replaced by just one or two men quietly hauling dredges and sorting the catch by hand. The lines of these gaff cutters have developed over the years and are distinctly Cornish in appearance. They have a long, deep keel and are straight of stem with a famously long bowsprit. The keel not only gives stability at sea, but also allows the oysterman to leave the helm occasionally to attend to his work.

One famous working boat is the distinctive *Victory*. Creamy-yellow coloured with striped tops'l, she was originally named *Royal Oak* and was built in 1884 by Frank Hitchens at Yard Point on one of the Fal's tributary creeks. She is just over 27 ft long and built of solid inch-thick pine on oak frames. She was acquired by the West family in 1925 to replace their quay punt lost in a wreck and, with the old boat's name, has remained with them until just recently, fishing by winter and racing in summer. *Victory* has undergone an extensive refit in the last few years which will ensure her presence in the regatta spectacles for another hundred.

winter Dig.

Working Punts

Often overshadowed by their more glamourous big sisters, the working punts of the west country deserve a second glance. They were sometimes the tenders to fishing boats and yachts, and would often be found tethered to the mooring while the men were at sea, or would be towed astern on passage. More than a humble transport, many of these boats made seaworthy fishing vessels in their own right. Working from quiet coves or right off rocky beaches, they were used for inspecting crab pots or for laying out a seine net. They would often sport a lug mains'l and sometimes a mizzen too.

A true survivor is the Falmouth dredging punt. Sometimes called 'winkboats', named after their hand winches, or 'haul-tow' punts, these 16 ft open boats are rowed to the shallower fishing grounds around the edge of the Carrick Roads. The oysterman deploys his dredge from one of two horizontal winches situated in the bows, while hauling in the anchor on the other. This is a scene that hasn't changed for hundreds of years. He sorts his catch on the stern thwart and, come late afternoon, heads for home once more.

Crabbers, toshers, and picarooners were bigger, heavier versions but built in just the same way – usually by eye or from simple frames and moulds, in sheds and fields near the creeks. They are still being built today and can be found nudging the harbour wall or bobbing on an out-haul as the tide turns.

TENDER = FOWEY

FALMOUTH DREDGING PUNT.

Falmouth Sunbeams

When one thinks of a yacht shape – sleek hull with shapely overhangs, tall triangular sails, two in number – perhaps the mighty J Class springs to mind, or may be the elegant Sunbeam. This 26 ft, 3 tonner is a true classic. Designed by Alfred Westmacott in 1922, she is regarded as a masterpiece not only to look at, but also to sail.

The Sunbeam class falls into two divisions: the Solent, and the Falmouth. Most boats were built by the firm of Woodnutt & Co Ltd of St Helens, Isle of Wight, but a few of the later ones were built by Curtis & Pape in Looe and most recently by craftsmen at Mylor Yacht Harbour overlooking the Fal. There have been only 45 Sunbeams to date, with one more in the Mylor workshop under construction. The two divisions are identical save one interesting feature. The Falmouth Sunbeams sport an 'original ingenious and effective device' known as the Kitty Gear. This is a piece of kit for booming out the jib on a run, whereas the Solent boats fly a more conventional spinnaker.

The Falmouth Sunbeams class was formed in 1924 by members of the Royal Cornwall Yacht Club. There were eight boats then and four more by 1937. After the war, the fleet grew in earnest to around eighteen today. Only one (on the Solent) has been lost to extreme weather.

Westmacott's specifications are strict and the list of materials comprehensive: keel – English elm; stem, deadwoods and horn timber – oak; planking – pitch pine; bent timbers – American elm; tiller – ash; etc; and all to be 'of the finest quality and the whole to be finished in the best workmanlike manner'. They are also to carry oars and rowlocks and a mop, though not all equipment is mandatory for racing!

While I was sketching, swallows darted in and out between the beams of the shed where this hull was taking shape – suitably dynamic stablemates for the beautiful craft that would grace many a startline with its swooping turns in years to come.

Falmouth Quay Punts

During the great days of sail, the port of Falmouth held special significance for the ocean-weary square riggers returning from the Far East, Australia and the Americas. They would have been at sea for many months carrying their cargoes, the life-blood of the empire. Falmouth was the first port of call in the English Channel and the last for outward bounders. It boasted a generous harbour, sheltered from most points, and a thriving support industry. Not least among the trades were the watermen who serviced the ships, with their no-nonsense quay punts.

The word 'punt' implies a little boat and the early ones were indeed only about 18 ft. They were open boats, lug rigged and low aspect. By the 1870s, however, competition had encouraged developments in design and a gaff yawl of around 30 ft became popular. They were still largely open but had a fore-deck back to the mast, plus side decks and afterlocker. The yawl enabled the boat to lower the main while on watch for trade, and jog easily with mizzen and stays'l. They were manoeuvrable and would sail alongside the towering ships right under their spreading yard arms. Their job was to fetch and carry fresh victuals and stores, tradesmen and shipwrights, and to transport passengers and of course mail and news. There was even the 'missionary boat' *Clarice*, offering more in the way of spiritual sustenance.

The yard of W E Thomas in Bar Creek was probably the most prolific in building quay punts, though there were others. His 26 ft *Pride of the Port* (pictured under winter rig) was reckoned to be one of the best. Like many others, she has not survived, but there are a few which have. One Thomas-built punt, *Louie Wills*, was recently discovered on the Thames and has been restored by Cornish craftsmen in Fowey. *Louie Wills* was built in 1900 and has had a checkered life, spending quite some time in Scotland and on London's river where she was found and finally bought by her present owner. He admits to a lifelong ambition to own a quay punt and has sailed her single-handed as far as Brest.

The Troys of Fowey

Many boats are designed and developed for their own patch of water. In the deep and sheltered port of Fowey, the indigenous species is the Troy class. Named after the book, *The History of Troy Town* by Sir Arthur Quiller Couch, this feisty 18 footer was originally designed as one that would be a consistent winner in the regattas. Sir Charles Hanson was looking for a boat for his daughter Clare, one in which she could compete successfully against Albert Bunt's *Maid of Foye*. At that time, the Fowey Sailing Club (FSC) had only one handicap class for open and half-decked boats. *Maid of Foye*, with her tops'l, dominated. Sir Charles approached local boat builder, Archie Watty, who had ideas of his own about fast boats. The manager of Lloyds Bank saw the new boat under construction and promptly ordered one for himself. Thus in the spring of 1929 two boats – Sir Charles's *Jocelyn* and Mr Strong's *Anemone* – were launched from Watty's shed at the end of Amity Court.

As fortune would have it, they didn't beat Mr Bunt over the line but, due to handicapping, *Jocelyn* proved to be reliably faster throughout the season and the fleet quickly grew to six. The FSC was persuaded to establish a class of their own and the Troys were born.

The early Troys were gunter rigged with long booms, though by 1934 the Troy owners decided to go for the Bermudan rig but using the same sails. The gunter has a virtually pointed gaff mains'l. This necessitated a mast of 30 ft above the deck. It's said that King George's sailing master, Sir Philip Hunloke, saw them racing in Plymouth Sound and recommended shortening the boom. His modifications were applied and we have the Troy of today, albeit with more modern terylene sails. The Troys still have their tall mast, said to be essential for catching the higher whiffles of wind in the steep valley.

Troys have proved adept travellers too. *Barbara* (T12), for instance, was taken to Padstow and, after the owner's death, to his nephew's home in Scotland! She actually sailed most of the way – around Land's End, up the Channel and the east coast to the Firth of Tay. Not bad for a tiny three-quarter decker. *Barbara* is now back in Fowey, her owners hoping to rebuild her in time for her 60th Birthday.

Anti-fouling Day

Polperro hooker, *Edith*, is one of possibly three hookers remaining, the other two being *Elizabeth Mary* (see page 36) and *Valda*, who was Plymouth-based until being sold recently to Northern Ireland. *Edith* was discovered in Falmouth by a previous owner and, though showing some obvious age, was thought worth restoring. There were signs that she was not a Falmouth boat: she was known to have fished and dredged for oysters on the Fal, and had been owned by the Ferris family of St Mawes for over seventy years, but her rig was shorter than most working boats, and she seemed to have a slot for a centre plate! Her wide transom stern also had a jumble of carved letters which defied translation. Further research revealed she was called *Edith of Fowey* and, because she was taken off the Fishing Register in 1895, possibly for a refit, was presumed to have been built in the latter part of the nineteenth century.

Other pointers, however, led to Polperro further along the coast. Photographs from the turn of the twentieth century show identical small fishing boats with big jack-yard tops'ls and three headsails on the long bowsprit. These boats were built in Looe by the two boat builders of the town, J Pearce and Oliver. They had a fish well and net hold amidships, and the shorter mast prevented too much roll at sea.

Edith has had a removable cabin fitted for a little cruising comfort, but the current owner prefers the open 'working' cockpit with a foredeck. There is space to occupy her young crew, and there's as much string to pull on the old gaffer now as when she was fishing for mullet and bass all those years ago.

Guide Me

Few boats stir as many emotions as *Guide Me*. She is both true survivor of a once great fishing tradition and a globe-trotting adventuress whose credentials read like romance. Built by P Ferris of Looe as a 40 ft mackerel drifter in 1911, *Guide Me* was one of the last of that breed to be built for sail and only had a tiny 4 hp engine fitted in 1917. She was registered in Fowey and worked the south Cornwall ports until being sold to an owner in the Channel Islands in 1968. Some time later she is known to have been in Southampton and Portsmouth and, when discovered by the Brickhill family, her current owners, was rotting on her beam ends in Fareham.

That was 1977 and the young couple were looking for a sailing home. Over the next ten years, *Guide Me* was steadily restored to her present configuration – dipping lugger and no engine. She has famously crossed the Atlantic from north to south and east to west, exploring anchorages in South Africa and South America. But then, as Judy Brickhill explains, these powerful fishing boats were designed to sail long distances as quickly as possible. Once at their fishing ground, the crews dropped the sails in order to work their drift nets. On the other side of the Channel, the Breton fishermen developed the standing lug which can be seen on the towering three-masted bisquines.

The Cornish luggers were far ranging, journeying from the western approaches below the Lizard, into the Irish Sea for herring and into the North Sea as far as Shetland. Some enterprising Cornishmen took full advantage of the sea-keeping abilities of their boats and sailed off to seek their fortunes in the southern hemisphere. Someone pointed out that you don't have to tack many times when you're going to Australia.

Standing on *Guide Me's* deck today, with her 40 ft unstayed masts and sails bent to the massive yards, it's not hard to imagine these ships at work. The simplicity of the rig is refreshing and the latent strength in the hull reassuring. Small wonder these boats once crossed oceans, and it will be no surprise when this one does again.

Shamrock

Shamrock was the last ketch to earn a living in the ports and harbours of the west country. She was built in the Stonehouse yard of Frederick Hawke in 1899 and was typical of the shallow draft sailing barges. These sturdy vessels were designed for working the creeks and rivers, often carrying stone from the quarries and other bulk cargoes (in *Shamrock's* case, her specialised trade was fertiliser). They were usually smack rigged with one mast but some, like *Shamrock*, were ketch rigged at one time or another. Two important features mark her out as special. Firstly, she was fitted with two drop keels, like a modern sailing dinghy, which improved her lateral resistance to the sea and improved her windward ability. Secondly, her shrouds were set up with the new bottle-screws as opposed to the traditional dead-eyes. It helped the crew in handling the masts.

In 1919 she was sold to a group of quarrymen and regularly made passages from Plymouth to Falmouth, and later carried stone from the quarries at Porthoustock to Tresillian on the Truro river. In the 1950s there was one other Tamar barge still working under sail and a few others with engines, but they have all gone, with the exception of the *Lynher*. *Shamrock* however was sold on in 1962. With two 65 hp diesels installed, she was used in salvage and prospecting before apparently ending her useful life as a scrap iron store in Hoo Lake off the river Plym where she was discovered by the National Maritime Museum.

A survey revealed that, though she was greatly worn by more than seventy years of hard work, renovation was a real option, and over the next few years Shamrock blossomed on the Tamar once more. She is now permanently berthed at The National Trust property of Cotehele, where you can visit this real gem of our maritime heritage. Some may even be lucky enough to see her under sail in Plymouth Sound on one of her rare trips to sea.

Garlandstone and Lynher

Garlandstone was the penultimate wooden merchantman to be built in the south of England. Her keel was laid in 1904 on the Devon side of the Tamar, opposite Calstock, in the yard of James Goss. She was steadily built up over the next four years as a 'spec' job, one that the yard would turn to when things were a bit quiet. James Goss was well known for his sailing barges, but he did build big trading ketches too. Finally launched in 1909, *Garlandstone* was successfully worked out of Milford Haven by her new owner, Captain John Russan. She had a paraffin engine installed in 1912 and the accommodation below decks was rearranged to fit.

There are detailed records of her busy life, her various owners, cargoes and ports of call. One notable skipper, Captain Alexander Murdoch, once sailed her back from Ireland to Lydney docks in Gloucester single handed! This was in the early stages of the Second World War, and it's said that he could find no crew to help him back, as they would have to skirt the edge of the Bristol Channel mine fields.

By the 1950s most of the great ketches had disappeared and few survive today. *Garlandstone* was bought by the National Museum of Wales and eventually 'chartered' to the Morwellham and Tamar Valley Trust where extensive restoration ensued. Thanks to the expert work undertaken, *Garlandstone* is now in perfect condition once more and permanently moored at the mining port of Morwellham, only a couple of miles from her birthplace beneath the viaduct at Calstock.

Lying alongside is the Tamar barge, *Lynher*. This remarkable boat has literally been brought back from the grave. She too was built by James Goss, in 1896 for the river trades which transported agricultural produce from the rich farmlands, ore, bricks, and limestone for kilns. *Lynher* carried quarried stone to Plymouth for the dockyards in the 1920s. By the '50s she was broken and abandoned, and left to sink slowly into the muddy river which shared her name. That's where Cornishman Charlie Force found her, fell for her and began to resurrect the rotting hulk. Once free of the sucking clay, she still floated and was eventually towed to Morwellham where, over the last few years, she has been restored. Today *Lynher* is cutter rigged and, although 51 ft long and able to carry 60 tonnes of cargo, she is said to row very well!

Max

Max is as pretty an example of an Edwardian launch as you'll find. She's a river boat and was built in the early twentieth century by E C (Teddy) Norris of Moricetown, Devonport. The yard was well known for its motor boats, often powered by Kelvin paraffin engines, and *Max* was no exception. Sadly though, precious few Norris launches have survived and the yard was destroyed by Second World War bombing.

The original engine was ruined in an early sinking and she spent many years powered by twin Seagull outboards. She had a short lug rig and oars to match. Her present owner Greg Powlesland saw *Max* at an auction in 1984 and bought her a short while later. Greg was also responsible for the restoration of *Marigold* at the same time and was looking for a boat to sail. Over the next few years Max was slowly brought back to her Edwardian style. An original Kelvin was acquired, new elm transom fitted and eventually smart new sails including gaff mains'l.

As a river boat, she has known a few mudbanks and experienced many happy picnics but, although designed for pottering, *Max* has proved an adept voyager too. Her skipper has sailed her to Fowey and Falmouth in testing conditions. They survived a broken rudder on one trip, and narrowly avoided colliding with a large turtle on another.

She is probably most at home exploring the deep, winding rivers and creeks of South Devon and Cornwall where she can be often found, still looking like a graceful image from a by-gone age.

Max

Max is as pretty an example of an Edwardian launch as you'll find. She's a river boat and was built in the early twentieth century by E C (Teddy) Norris of Moricetown, Devonport. The yard was well known for its motor boats, often powered by Kelvin paraffin engines, and *Max* was no exception. Sadly though, precious few Norris launches have survived and the yard was destroyed by Second World War bombing.

The original engine was ruined in an early sinking and she spent many years powered by twin Seagull outboards. She had a short lug rig and oars to match. Her present owner Greg Powlesland saw *Max* at an auction in 1984 and bought her a short while later. Greg was also responsible for the restoration of *Marigold* at the same time and was looking for a boat to sail. Over the next few years Max was slowly brought back to her Edwardian style. An original Kelvin was acquired, new elm transom fitted and eventually smart new sails including gaff mains'l.

As a river boat, she has known a few mudbanks and experienced many happy picnics but, although designed for pottering, *Max* has proved an adept voyager too. Her skipper has sailed her to Fowey and Falmouth in testing conditions. They survived a broken rudder on one trip, and narrowly avoided colliding with a large turtle on another.

She is probably most at home exploring the deep, winding rivers and creeks of South Devon and Cornwall where she can be often found, still looking like a graceful image from a by-gone age.

Bessie Ellen

Across the Cattewater, the estuary of the river Plym, lies the picturesque village of Turnchapel. Still a quiet backwater compared with Plymouth, this is where William Kelly's shipyard was situated. Here in 1904 he laid the keel of a ketch that would be finished four years later and christened *Bessie Ellen* by the eponymous daughters of her proud new owner, John Chichester of Barnstaple. The story goes he produced a bag of gold sovereigns, telling his son Jack, 'I don't suppose you have seen them before, and I doubt you will ever see them again.' The bag went back in his pocket until his arrival at the yard where he laid them on the table, thus paying for his ship.

Bessie Ellen proved a fast and seaworthy working ship, although an accident in 1910 made her leak on and off for years. Like many of her peers, she had an antiquated engine fitted and her elegant rig was reduced in 1917. There was competition from steamers and work would have been hard, especially with a short-handed crew of three. Tragically, Captain Chichester was killed, crushed in an accident by a barge entering Sharpness docks and, though several skippers acted as master, John's widow, Bessie, continued to run the business.

The advent of the Second World War heralded the death of working sail. Many ships were commandeered for war use and then abandoned as lack of funds made re-commissioning impractical. *Bessie* survived though, and was bought by a Dane for the Baltic trades. Renamed *Forsøget* (The Attempt) she was worked hard up to the 1970s until she eventually became unprofitable. She was bought by the enthusiastic Ole Pietersen who undertook restoration of the shapely hull. His limited funds and lack of youth counted against the project, however, and she was put up for sale, where she stayed for twenty years until her current owner bought her. She completed a great deal of work at the Danish yard of J Ring Andersen before being brought home to Plymouth once more. *Bessie Ellen* is now berthed along the Cattewater wharfs, less than a mile from where she was built. Engulfed by a huge purpose-built tent, her decks resemble a building site at the moment but owner Nikki Alford is aiming that *Bessie* will sail and earn her keep as a working charter ship well into the next century.

Marigold

Looking at *Marigold* today, it's hard to imagine her as a derelict, languishing not that long ago in a mud berth in the upper reaches of a salt creek. Indeed she is mentioned in a book of wrecks. Designed and built in 1892 by Nicholson's at Gosport, she was an elegant gentleman's yacht in the halcyon days of big boat sailing. She was raced successfully in those early years and, though little is known from 1915 to 1930, she was probably moored in Essex and laid up for the duration of the First World War. With the development of the Bermudan rig in the late 1920s *Marigold* was converted to the more modern rig with its high aspect triangular mains'l.

Marigold's logbook from this period features many famous faces, including a youthful David Niven. Though it is clear that other changes were made to her original layout, these photographs proved a valuable source of reference in her future restoration. By the 1960s she was an old boat and needed much attention. One owner took her to the Hamble, converted her to a schooner and sailed her on till 1972. By 1982 she was derelict and in danger of demolition when spotted by Greg Powlesland, who began the mammoth labour of love which restored *Marigold* to her former glory.

Marigold was transported to Cornwall to be slowly reborn beneath the piers of the old railway bridge near the river Lynher. The catalogue of works was daunting. She was sold to yachtsman Mr G Allan for completion and Greg was retained to manage the project. Timbers and planking were gradually replaced, the deck was renewed and new bronze floors replaced the old corroded iron. The story is well documented but it must be said that she is one of the most authentic restorations afloat and, during the extensive rebuild, every detail was researched. From the deck fittings to the leather button upholstery, *Marigold* is a model of Edwardian yachting.

To be overhauled by this yacht is an experience. As you glance up at the towering acres of canvas and the sleek black hull, you have to admit *Marigold* is just a bit special.

Elizabeth Mary

Originally built by R Pearce in Looe in 1909, *Elizabeth Mary* has had a varied life fishing and carrying as a Polperro hooker. From 1920 she was owned by a sailing school and from 1965 to 1970 dredged for oysters on the Fal. She has also been known to have once moored on the Dart and the Tamar.

The hookers worked out of most of the south coast ports – Looe, Dartmouth, Brixham and Plymouth. They fell into two classes: those around 40 ft, fully decked with a standing lug on a mizzen, and smaller inshore boats, around 30 ft, straight stemmed, transom sterned, and cutter rigged with a fore deck like many other typical west country working boats. Some worked as long-liners way outside the Eddystone and their long, deep keels, developed for the channel swells, have spawned numerous imitators today. Strangely, few of these robust craft survive. A few were converted to engine power and can be spotted alongside harbour walls, but many have simply disappeared. There is interest once more, however, in the humble hooker and at least one has been built recently.

Elizabeth Mary is half-decked and, although she looks as if she'd be cramped below, there is a remarkable amount of headroom in the dim and ropy smelling fore-peak. A heavily built working boat, she still displays her Plymouth registration of PH 107. Here she is chasing my own Percy Dalton designed Falmouth working boat, *Sadie Dalton*. The more modern boat's taller rig and finer lines ensure a win as they beat across the western end of Plymouth Sound in light airs towards Devil's Point.

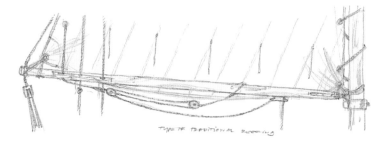

Salcombe Yawls

When you look closely at the shining hull of a new Salcombe yawl, it's hard to imagine this refined 16 footer as a fishing boat. The hardened racer did in fact develop from the long-liners that chased shoals of mackerel in the 1920s and '30s. They would set out with all three sails aloft, but once at their chosen fishing ground the crew would lower the main and trim the boat under jib and mizzen. These were open boats with the main mast well forward and the mizzen stepped on a bracket outside the transom. Once work was done, it would be up main and head for home, taking care to avoid any white water on the notorious Salcombe bar.

As the century wore on, so the racing aspect of these dinghies evolved. Fishing declined and, as elsewhere, modern motor boats illustrated an edge of efficiency over the little yawls. In the last fifteen or twenty years, with the development of sailing for leisure, the design of the racing yawl has reached new peaks. Many owners now keep their boats for competition only.

There was never really a set of lines for the class and each boat conformed to an ideal rather than to a rating. Recently, though, several new yawls have been built by boatbuilder Mike Atfield to a design by international yacht designer Ian Howlett. These have proved highly successful in the summer regattas and Mike has orders for more. They are made of wood, specifically mahogany on oak timbers and copper fastened throughout. Their masts and spars are wood and the centreplates are bronze. There are some very modern looking fittings on deck but, as Mike is quick to point out, the Salcombe yawl is still a very traditional boat.

Tomboy

Tomboy and *Guide Me* rest on their legs after being moved down stream on the spring tide. On two occasions I have watched *Tomboy* work her way in to busy harbours under sail. Her young skipper expertly employs skills that most modern yachtsmen have never heard of. Many of them will not go to sea without an engine, but the absence of the 'iron tops'l' is no handicap to *Tomboy* and she is a familiar visitor to ports on both sides of the western approaches.

She was built in 1912 by W J Hodges in a yard situated just above Higher Ferry on the Dart. The yard built a number of working boats for the south Devon fishery based at Brixham, but Hodges also built several yachts for members of the Royal Torbay Yacht Club, just over the hills on the coast, and *Tomboy* was one of them. She is typically of the period, plumb stemmed and counter sterned, and constructed of larch on oak. She has a long bowsprit and equally long boom behind the mast, giving an overall air of balance and harmony. Like many older boats, she needed some 'TLC' to make her seaworthy and much hard work has gone into refastening the hull, laying a new deck and fitting a new oak stempost.

Tomboy is also now rigged as nature intended. Many Edwardian yachts succumbed to the Bermudan style in the intervening years but, thanks to the 'revival' of the gaff rig, some are kicking up their petticoats beneath four-sided sails once again. There are lots of other pretty yachts from the turn of the last century and, thanks to enthusiastic owners and sympathetic craftsmen, they are still sailing – and, in the case of *Tomboy*, still collecting trophies.

Little Mint

ittle Mint is the only surviving Mumble Bee sailing trawler and, although built in Looe in 1913, was always based in Brixham. She was the last purpose-built cutter operating for the Brixham fishery. The name for these hardy vessels was coined because of their fishing for oysters on the Mumbles Bank off Swansea. The beds were free to all and attracted boats from as far away as the east coast.

Little Mint has had an eventful life. She had an engine fitted in the 1920s and in 1938 was accidentally sunk on her moorings by a Belgian trawler! She was raised and repaired, and continued to work through the Second World War, carrying cargo such as paraffin. *Little Mint* took part in the Dunkirk expedition, although she turned back when the skipper heard of a missing crew member from another small boat. They successfully picked up the elderly sailor and returned to Brixham. Later in the war, she came across a German submarine on the surface and prepared to ram it, making the enemy dive to escape! She also survived attack from enemy aircraft and machine guns.

After the war, *Little Mint* continued to fish until 1955, after moving to Newhaven in 1950. Later she retired to a cruising life and, following a hefty rebuild in Suffolk from 1994 to 1995, her current owner brought her back to the south coast where she can be found sailing for pleasure the fishing grounds of her youth.

Brixham Trawlers

*L*eader and *Provident* surge down channel with every stitch aloft. The trawlers of Brixham were probably the most powerful sailing fishing boats in Europe during the late years of the nineteenth century. Indeed no other vessel could tow the heavy trawls and carry their catch so swiftly back to port. There is evidence of a sizeable fleet working the Skerries Bank from the 1770s. As markets developed, the smaller cutters were replaced by the great ketches. Some were cut in half and lengthened to accommodate the mizzen and larger gear. These big boats could easily make longer passages and their design inspired similar trawlers to be built, especially in the north of England. Many Devon fishermen settled in ports such as Lowestoft, Grimsby and Scarborough.

The advent of new technology brought the advantage of steam winches to haul the heavy trawls and, though many sailing fleets were replaced by steamers, some efficient Brixham trawlers continued to work right up to the eve of the Second World War.

Both *Leader* and *Provident* were built in the same yard on the banks of the Dart at Galmpton. W A Gibbs launched the 110 ft LOA (length overall) *Leader* in 1892 for one William Robbens of Lowestoft. She worked out of that port until 1907 when she was sold to a Swedish company. There she continued as a trawler until 1953 and then as a cargo vessel, still under sail. In 1969 the Swedish Cruising Association restored her after a hard-working life, and she started a new career in sail training and chartering. By the mid 1980s, and renamed *Lorne Leader*, she was based in western Scotland.

Now alongside her sisters, *Provident* and *Golden Vanity* (also built at Galmpton), she is finally based at Brixham and owned by charter and sail training company, Trinity Sailing, which offers willing crews the chance to experience the thrill of handling one of our mighty sailing trawlers.

Beer Luggers

There is a saying in south Devon that Beer made Brixham and Brixham made the North Sea. The stony beach at Beer looks an improbable place to start a legend, but it's often the way. Alan Abbott, founder of the Beer Luggers Club, says it's likely that local men worked from Brixham when the weather was too bad to launch on the exposed beach at Beer. The little luggers of today are essentially summer racers, their ancestry stretching back generations to when mackerel liners, herring drifters and trawlers all worked off the surf-pounded shingle below the cliffs. It still looks precarious, but the lugger men made an art of working off the beach.

Boats have been launched at Beer for a thousand years and quite big luggers worked there well into the twentieth century. There are photographs of three masted, clinker-built vessels with their distinctive rig before the First World War. Beer luggers were basically open boats with scant shelter beneath a cuddy in the bows. Their trademark iron bumkin, with two or three hooks for the tack of the fore-lug, sloped stiffly downwards from the upper stem, and the tall luff was held to windward by a spar called a fore-guard or fore-girt. There is a rare photograph of the *Beatrice Anne* with the full rig in action. Clearly visible are the oar ports known as tomkin holes in the plank below the sheer strake. The boats were man-handled up and down the beach, the larger ones, some up to 30 ft in length, being hauled by the hand capstan that still overlooks the bay. The last big lugger was broken up in 1935 as engines again took over from sail, but the lines of one, the auxiliary *Little Jim* built by Lavis of Exmouth, were taken at that time.

Even by modern racing standards the Beer luggers do carry a lot of canvas and, being shallow draughted, are said to be 'a little lively'. Most continue to have been clinker-built and date from the 1950s, though lighter fibreglass is making an appearance. The distinctive rig is unchanged and their red sails still contrast with the blue of Lyme Bay on a summer's day.